A Father's Journey

Published by Lulu and Bell
ISBN: 978-1-83990-437-0
Lulu and Bell 2024

Contents

How to use this guided journal	1 - 3
Childhood: The Beginning	4 - 12
Childhood: The Early Years	13 - 25
Childhood: Teenage Years	26 - 35
Young Adulthood	36 - 51
Friendships and Relationships	52 - 62
Special Events	63 - 73
Fatherhood	74 - 83
Reflections	84 - 96
Quick- Fire Questions	97

How to use this guided journal

Using this guided journal is an excellent way to explore and tell the story of your life. It provides structure, inspiration, and guidance as you reflect on and document your experiences, thoughts, and emotions. Here's a step-by-step description of how to use this guided journal effectively:

Set a Regular Writing Routine

Dedicate a specific time and place for journaling. Consistency is key. Set aside a few minutes each day or a specific day of the week to engage with your guided journal. Find a quiet and comfortable space where you can focus without distractions.

Read the Prompts Carefully

Take the time to read and understand the prompts provided in your guided journal. Prompts can range from specific questions about your childhood or pivotal life events to broader themes like personal growth or aspirations. Make sure you comprehend each prompt before responding.

Reflect and Write

Allow yourself to reflect on the prompt before putting pen to paper. Consider the memories, emotions, and insights associated with the prompt. Think about how the prompt relates to your life story and what aspects you'd like to highlight. When you're ready, begin writing your response. Be honest, authentic, and delve deep into your thoughts and experiences.

Be Open

Allow yourself to express both the joys and challenges of your life. Explore your triumphs, failures, lessons learned, and the growth you've experienced along the way. Writing authentically will help you capture the essence of your life story.

Add Details and Context

As you respond to the prompts, include specific details, anecdotes, and memories that add depth to your story. Describe the people, places, and events that have shaped your life. This will create a vivid and engaging narrative that showcases your unique experiences.

Review and Reflect

Periodically review your previous entries to gain a broader perspective on your life story. Reflect on the connections and patterns you observe. This can provide valuable insights into your personal growth, values, and aspirations.

Customize and Personalize

Don't be afraid to customize your guided journal experience. Add your own prompts, illustrations, or photographs to make it uniquely yours. This personal touch will further enrich your storytelling journey.

Embrace the Journey

Remember, telling the story of your life is a process that unfolds over time. Embrace the journey and enjoy the self-discovery and reflection that comes with it. Don't rush through the prompts but allow yourself to fully explore and express your narrative.

By following these steps, you'll be able to effectively use a guided journal with prompts to tell the story of your life. It can be a fulfilling and introspective experience that allows you to gain a deeper understanding of yourself and your journey.

Childhood: The Beginning

Can you describe the day you were born and any special memories your parents or family shared with you?

_____
_____
_____
_____
_____
_____
_____
_____
_____
_____
_____
_____
_____
_____
_____
_____
_____
_____
_____
_____
_____
_____
_____
_____

Did your parents or family share any memories of you as a baby?

Is there any significance or story behind your name?

_____
_____
_____
_____
_____
_____
_____
_____

Where did you spend the first few years of your life, and what was your home like during that time?

_____
_____
_____
_____
_____
_____
_____
_____

Can you share any significant milestones or accomplishments you achieved during your early years?

Were there any significant historical events or cultural changes happening around the world during your early years that you remember?

What were some of your favorite toys, comfort objects or games to play with as a young child?

_____

_____

_____

_____

_____

_____

_____

Have you been told of any funny or adorable things you said or did as a toddler?

_____

_____

_____

_____

_____

_____

_____

Were there any specific books, songs or bedtime stories that you loved hearing over and over again?

Did you go to any groups and have any play friends?

Childhood: The Early Years

What are some of your earliest memories from your childhood?

_____
_____
_____
_____
_____
_____
_____
_____
_____
_____
_____
_____
_____
_____
_____
_____
_____
_____
_____
_____
_____
_____
_____
_____
_____
_____
_____

Where did you grow up and what was it like living there?

Did you have any favorite games or activities that you enjoyed as a child?

_____
_____
_____
_____
_____
_____
_____
_____

What were your favorite subjects or hobbies in school?

_____
_____
_____
_____
_____
_____
_____
_____
_____
_____

Can you tell me about any special traditions or celebrations your family had when you were growing up?

_____

_____

_____

_____

_____

_____

_____

Did you have any siblings, and what was your relationship with them like?

_____

_____

_____

_____

_____

_____

_____

_____

_____

What were your parents like? How would you describe your relationship with them?

Did you have any chores or responsibilities around the house when you were young?

_____
_____
_____
_____
_____
_____
_____

What were some of the challenges or hardships you faced during your childhood?

_____
_____
_____
_____
_____
_____
_____
_____
_____
_____

Were there any memorable vacations or trips that you went on with your family?

Were there any memorable friendships or relationships you had during that time?

___

Do you remember any special birthday parties or celebrations during this time?

___

Do you have any pets growing up and what were they like?

___

___

___

___

___

___

___

Were there any specific books, movies, or songs that were popular or influential during your childhood?

___

___

___

___

___

___

___

___

___

Is there anything you wish you could have done differently or any lessons you learned during your childhood that shaped who you are today?

Childhood: Teenage Years

What was your favorite part about being a teenager?

_____
_____
_____
_____
_____
_____
_____
_____
_____
_____
_____
_____
_____
_____
_____
_____
_____
_____
_____
_____
_____

Can you describe your high school experience? What were some memorable moments or events?

_____
_____
_____
_____
_____
_____
_____

Who were your closest friends during your teenage years? Are you still in touch with them?

_____
_____
_____
_____
_____
_____
_____
_____
_____

Did you participate in any extracurricular activities or clubs in school?
What were they, and what did you enjoy about them?

_____
_____
_____
_____
_____
_____
_____

What were your favorite fashion trends or styles when you were a teenager?

_____
_____
_____
_____
_____
_____
_____
_____
_____
_____

Did you have any part-time jobs or responsibilities during your teenage years? How did they influence your life?

_____
_____
_____
_____
_____
_____
_____

Were there any significant hobbies or interests that you developed during your teenage years?

_____
_____
_____
_____
_____
_____
_____
_____
_____

Can you recall any special trips or vacations you took during this time? What made them memorable?

Were there any particular music artists, bands, or songs that you loved during your teenage years?

_____
_____
_____
_____
_____
_____
_____

What were some of the challenges or struggles you faced as a teenager, and how did you overcome them?

_____
_____
_____
_____
_____
_____
_____
_____
_____

Did you have any favorite books or movies that made a significant impact on you during that time?

___

What were your aspirations or dreams for the future when you were a teenager?

___

Can you describe your relationship with your parents during your teenage years? How did it evolve?

Is there any advice or lessons learned from your teenage years that you would like to share with me?

Young Adulthood

Can you describe what your life was like when you first entered adulthood after finishing high school?

What were your career aspirations or goals during your young adulthood? Did they change over time?

Did you pursue higher education or attend college/university? If so, what did you study, and how did that experience shape you?

_____
_____
_____
_____
_____
_____
_____
_____
_____
_____
_____
_____
_____
_____
_____
_____
_____
_____
_____
_____
_____
_____
_____

Can you share any memorable moments or achievements from your early career or professional life?

_____
_____
_____
_____
_____
_____
_____

Did you live on your own or with roommates during your young adulthood? How did that experience impact you?

_____
_____
_____
_____
_____
_____
_____
_____
_____
_____

Did you have any specific hobbies or interests that you were passionate about during this time?

___

What were some of the biggest challenges or obstacles you faced during your early adult years, and how did you overcome them?

___

Can you recall any significant relationships or romantic experiences you had during your young adulthood?

How did you manage your finances and
navigate financial independence during
your young adulthood?

_____

_____

_____

_____

_____

_____

_____

Were there any pivotal life events or experiences that
significantly shaped your perspective or values during this
time?

_____

_____

_____

_____

_____

_____

_____

_____

_____

_____

Can you share any travels or adventures you embarked on during your young adulthood?

What were some of the lessons or wisdom you gained from your experiences during this period of your life?

_____

_____

_____

_____

_____

_____

_____

Did you have any mentors or role models who influenced you during your young adulthood?

_____

_____

_____

_____

_____

_____

_____

_____

_____

_____

_____

Looking back, is there any advice you would give to your younger self during this time?

Friendships and Relationships

Can you tell me about your closest friends during different stages of your life? What made those friendships special?

Can you share any stories or memories about your best friend(s) during your younger years?

_____
_____
_____
_____
_____
_____
_____

What were some of the qualities or characteristics you valued in your friends and romantic partners when you were younger?

_____
_____
_____
_____
_____
_____
_____
_____
_____
_____

How did you meet your significant other? Can you share any stories about how your relationship developed?

Can you recall any memorable dates, trips, or experiences you had with your significant other?

Did you ever experience heartbreak or significant challenges in your relationships? How did you navigate through those difficult times?

_____
_____
_____
_____
_____
_____
_____

Were there any friendships or relationships that had a significant impact on your life or shaped who you are today?

_____
_____
_____
_____
_____
_____
_____
_____
_____
_____

Can you share any lessons or insights you gained from your friendships and relationships in the past?

_____
_____
_____
_____
_____
_____
_____
_____

Did you ever have a long-distance relationship or maintain friendships from afar? How did you manage to stay connected?

_____
_____
_____
_____
_____
_____
_____
_____
_____
_____

How did your friendships and relationships change as you entered different phases of your life, such as starting a family or pursuing a career?

Can you share any funny or heartwarming anecdotes about your friends or romantic partners?

Special Events

Can you tell me about your wedding day? What were the most memorable moments or details?

_____
_____
_____
_____
_____
_____
_____
_____
_____
_____
_____
_____
_____
_____
_____
_____
_____
_____
_____
_____
_____
_____
_____
_____
_____

Did you have any milestone birthdays or celebrations that hold a special place in your heart? Can you describe them?

_____
_____
_____
_____
_____
_____
_____

Can you share any stories or memories from family reunions or gatherings that were particularly meaningful or fun?

_____
_____
_____
_____
_____
_____
_____
_____
_____
_____

Did you have any major achievements or accomplishments that you celebrated? How did you commemorate those moments?

Can you recall any vacations or trips that stand out as unforgettable experiences? What made them so special?

Have you ever attended a significant cultural or religious event that left a lasting impression on you? Can you describe it?

___

___

___

___

___

___

___

___

Did you have the opportunity to witness any historical events or be a part of any social movements? How did those events impact you?

___

___

___

___

___

___

___

___

___

___

___

Can you describe any special anniversaries or milestone moments in your relationship with your significant other?

Did you have the chance to meet any influential or famous individuals throughout your life? Who were they, and what was that experience like?

_____
_____
_____
_____
_____
_____
_____

Can you share any stories or memories from graduation ceremonies or academic achievements that were important to you?

_____
_____
_____
_____
_____
_____
_____
_____
_____

Have you ever experienced a moment of personal growth or self-discovery that you consider a special event in your life?

Fatherhood

What were your initial thoughts and emotions when you found out you were going to become a father?

_____
_____
_____
_____
_____
_____
_____
_____
_____
_____
_____
_____
_____
_____
_____
_____
_____
_____
_____
_____
_____
_____
_____

What were some of the biggest challenges you faced during the early stages and how did you overcome them?

_____
_____
_____
_____
_____
_____
_____
_____

How did your perspective on life and your priorities change after becoming a father?

_____
_____
_____
_____
_____
_____
_____
_____
_____
_____

Did you have any specific parenting philosophies or approaches that guided you in fatherhood?

_____
_____
_____
_____
_____
_____
_____

What were the most rewarding aspects of being a father for you?

_____
_____
_____
_____
_____
_____
_____
_____
_____

Were there any times when you felt unsure or overwhelmed as a father? How did you navigate those moments?

_____
_____
_____
_____
_____
_____
_____

How did your relationship with your own parents or family change after becoming a father?

_____
_____
_____
_____
_____
_____
_____
_____

Can you share any important life lessons or values that you wanted to instill as a parent?

What are some of the things you have learned or discovered about yourself through the journey of fatherhood?

_____
_____
_____
_____
_____
_____
_____
_____
_____
_____
_____
_____
_____
_____
_____
_____
_____
_____
_____
_____
_____
_____
_____
_____

Reflections

How do you feel when you look back on your life as a whole?

_____
_____
_____
_____
_____
_____
_____
_____
_____
_____
_____
_____
_____
_____
_____
_____
_____
_____
_____
_____
_____
_____
_____
_____

What are some of the biggest lessons you've learned throughout your life journey?

_____
_____
_____
_____
_____
_____
_____
_____
_____
_____
_____
_____
_____
_____
_____
_____
_____
_____
_____
_____
_____
_____
_____
_____

If you could go back and change one thing about your past, what would it be and why?

___

What are some of the most important values or principles that have guided you throughout your life?

___

Can you identify any significant turning points or pivotal moments that shaped the course of your life?

_____
_____
_____
_____
_____
_____
_____

How do you think your priorities and perspectives have evolved over the years?

_____
_____
_____
_____
_____
_____
_____
_____
_____
_____

Are there any regrets or missed opportunities that you wish you had pursued differently?

_____
_____
_____
_____
_____
_____
_____

Can you reflect on the challenges or hardships you've faced and how they have contributed to your personal growth?

_____
_____
_____
_____
_____
_____
_____
_____
_____
_____

What are some of the most cherished memories or accomplishments from your life that bring you joy?

How do you feel about the relationships and connections you've formed with family, friends, and loved ones over the years?

Have you achieved the goals and dreams you had envisioned for yourself when you were younger? How do you feel about them now?

_____
_____
_____
_____
_____
_____
_____

How do you hope to be remembered by those who have known you throughout your life?

_____
_____
_____
_____
_____
_____
_____
_____
_____

Can you share any wisdom or advice you would give to your younger self if you had the chance?

What are you most grateful for when you look back on your life?

Quick-Fire Questions

What's your favorite book?
_____
_____

What's your favorite movie?
_____
_____

Coffee or tea?
_____

Cats or dogs?
_____

Beach or mountains?
_____

Sweet or savory?
_____

Early bird or night owl?
_____

What's your favorite color?
_____

What's your favorite season?
_____

What's your favorite song?
_____
_____

www.ingramcontent.com/pod-product-compliance
Lightning Source LLC
LaVergne TN
LVHW071521161224
799242LV00008B/93